Discovering Biblical Treasures

UNDERSTANDING RUTH

A commentary using Ancient Bible Study Methods

Michael Harvey Koplitz

This edition copyright ©2019. Michael H. Koplitz.

All rights reserved. No part of this publication may be reproduced or transmitted in any form or by any means without permission of the publisher.

All Scripture quotations, unless otherwise noted, are taken from the New American Standard Bible®, Copyright © 1960, 1962, 1963, 1968, 1971, 1972, 1973, 1975, 1977, 1995 by the Lockman Foundation. Used by permission. (www.Lockman.org)

The NASB uses italic to indicate words that have been added for clarification. Citations are shown with large capital letters.

Published by Michael H. Koplitz

Acknowledgment

This work could not have been accomplished without Dr. Anne Davis, who taught me Ancient (Hebraic) Bible study methods, and my two study partners, Rev. Dr. Robert Cook and Pastor Sandra Koplitz. We know that the journey has just started and will last a lifetime. The discovery of the depths of God's Word is waiting for us to find.

Table of Contents

Introduction

While I was attending Seminary earning my M. Div. degree, I started to question what the instructors and reference books were saying about the Scriptures. One of the ideas being offered then was that the Bible was full of errors and not factual. I found that attitude disturbing for Seminary instructors to be teaching. After all, the Seminary experience is to train pastors to go out into God's world and preach the Bible. How can you preach the Bible if you believe what these instructors are teaching? The methods that were being taught to examine the Bible just seemed inaccurate to me.

After graduating from Seminary, I spent a lot of time reading different views about the Bible. I eventually read the Zohar. This collection of midrashim is considered the secret work of the Torah, according to Kabbalists. In addition, I read quite a bit about Messianic Judaism. Their view of the Bible is quite different than the Seminary view.

I decided that the biblical interpretation that was being taught in Seminary was not the biblical interpretation the people heard when Jesus Christ (whose Hebraic name is Yeshua) preached. I went on a quest to learn what the people of Yeshua's day thought about Scripture, and what they thought when the Scriptures were read. This quest led me to Dr. Anne Davis and The Bible Learning University. Dr. Davis was in search of the same thing I was searching. She had made many discoveries that helped me in my quest. I earned the Ph. D. degree from The Bible Learning University in Hebraic Studies in Christianity concentrating on ancient Bible Studies methods.

Finally, I found someone who believed that the church has placed almost 1900 years of their theological ideas about the Scriptures and in many places possibly distorting its original meaning. What is also important to hear is that the basic tenants of Yeshua as God's Messiah, my Lord and Savior are in the Bible. My faith in Yeshua is stronger now that I have learned from Dr. Davis how to study the Scriptures in the same manner that the people did in Yeshua's day.

I have included an article that describes the differences between Greek learning methods and Hebraic learning methods. Please do not skip this chapter unless you are familiar with ancient Bible study methods because if you do, then the analysis and commentary that follows may become difficult for you to understand.

Our God is vast and infinite, and so is His Word. May God bless you in your discovery of what God's Word is about.

The book of Ruth is a simple folktale which was scribed in an uncomplicated style. Ruth and Naomi were simple poor persons. An Israelite and a Moabite (a descendant of Lot) who came together and became important in Israel's history because Ruth became the great-great-grandmother of King David.

The book teaches about inner values of kindness and the power of love. The value of faith in the LORD and family life is shown to be sacred.[1]

---

[1] Rocco A. Errico and George M. Lamsa, *Aramaic Light on Joshua Through 2 Chronicles* (Smyrna: GA: Noohra Foundation, 2009).

The main differences between the Greek method and the Hebraic method of teaching

Once a student becomes aware of these two teaching styles, the student will be able to determine if the class attended or if a book read, whether the teaching method is either a Greek or Hebraic method. In the Greek manner, the instructor is always right because of advanced knowledge. In the college situation, it is because the professor has his/her Ph.D. in some area of study, so one assumes that he or she knows everything about the topic. For example, Rodney Dangerfield played the role of a middle-aged man going to college. His English midterm was to write about Kurt Vonnegut Jr. Since he did not understand any of Vonnegut's books he hired Vonnegut himself to write the midterm. When he received the paper from the English Professor told Dangerfield that whoever wrote the paper knew nothing about Vonnegut. The professor's words are an example of the Greek method of teaching. Did the Ph.D. English professor think that she knew more about Vonnegut's writings than Vonnegut did? [2]

---

[2] *Back to School.* Performed by Rodney Dangerfield. Hollywood: CA: Paper Clip Productions, 1986. DVD.

In the Greek teaching method, the professor or the instructor claims to be the authority. If one attends a Bible study class and the class leader says, "I will teach you the only way to understand this biblical book," you may want to consider the implications. This method is standard since most Seminaries and Bible colleges teach a Greek mode of learning, which is the same method the church has been utilizing for centuries.

Hebraic teaching methods are different. The teacher wants the students to challenge what they hear. It is through questioning that a student can learn. Also, the teacher wants his/her students to excel to a point where the student becomes the teacher.

If two rabbis come together to discuss a passage of Scripture, the result will be at least ten different opinions. All points of view are acceptable if each is supported by biblical evidence. It is permissible and encouraged that students develop many ideas. There is a depth to God's Word, and God wants us to find all His messages contained in the Scripture.

Seeking out the meaning of the Scriptures beyond the literal meaning is essential to understand God's Word fully.[3] The Greek method of learning the Scriptures has prevailed over the centuries. One problem is that only the literal interpretation of Scripture was often viewed as valid, as prompted by Martin Luther's "sola literalis" meaning that just the literal translation of Scripture was accurate. The Fundamentalist movements of today base their beliefs on the literal interpretation of the Scripture. Therefore, they do not believe that God placed more profound, hidden, or secret meanings in the Word.

The students of the Scriptures who learn through Hebraic training and understanding have drawn a different conclusion. The Hebrew language itself leads to different possible interpretations because of the construction of the language. The Hebraic method of Bible study opens avenues of thought about God's revelations in the Scripture never considered. Not all questions about the Scripture studied will have an immediate answer. If so, it becomes the responsibility of the learners to

---

[3] Davis, Anne Kimball. *The Synoptic Gospels*. MP3. Albuquerque: NM: BibleInteract, 2012.

uncover the meaning. Also, remember that many opinions about the meaning of Scripture are also acceptable.

Methodology

The methodology employed is to use First Century Scripture study methods integrated with the customs and culture of Yeshua's day to examine the Hebrew and Christian Scriptures, thus gathering a more in-depth understanding by learning the Scriptures in the way the people of Yeshua's day did.

I have titled the methodology of analyzing a passage of Scripture in a Hebraic manner the "Process of Discovery." The author developed this methodology which brings together the various areas of linguistic and cultural understanding. There are several sections to the process and not all the parts apply to every passage of Scripture. The overall result of developing this process is to give the reader a framework for studying the word in more depth.

The "Process of Discovery" starts with a Scripture passage. An examination of the linguistic structure of the passage is next. The linguistic structure includes parallelism, chiastic structures, and repetition. Formatting the passage in its linguistic form allows the reader to be able to visualize what the first century CE listener was hearing. Their corresponding sections label the chiasms, for example, A, B, C, B', A.' Not all passages of the Scriptures have a poetic form.

The next step is to "question the narrative." The questioning the narrative process assuming the reader knows nothing about the passage. Therefore, the questions go from the simple to the complex. The next task is to identify any linguistic patterns. Linguistic patterns include, but are not limited to irony, simile, metaphor, symbolism, idioms, hyperbole, figurative language, personification, and allegory.

A review of any translation inconsistencies discovered between the English NAU version and either the Hebrew or Greek versions is done. There are times when a Hebrew or Greek word is translated in more than one way. Inconsistencies also can be created by the translation committee, which may have decided to use traditional language instead of the actual translation. The decision of the translation committee is in the Preface or Introduction to the Bible. Perhaps some of the inconsistencies were intentionally added to convey some deeper meaning. An examination for every discrepancy is done.

The passage is analyzed for any echoes of the Hebrew Scriptures in the Christian Scriptures. Using a passage from the Hebrew Scriptures in the Christian Scriptures, an echo occurs.[4] Also, echoes are found when Torah (Genesis through Deuteronomy) passages are used in other Hebrew Bible books. Cross-references in the Scripture are references from one verse to another verse which can assist the reader in understanding the verse.

The names of persons mentioned in the passage are listed. Many of the Hebrew names have meaning and may be associated with places or actions. Jewish parents used to name their children based on what they felt God had in store for their child. An example of this is Abraham whose original name was Abram and was changed to mean eternal father (God changed Abram's name to Abraham indicating a function he was to perform). When the Hebrew Bible gives names, many of the occurrences mean something unique. The same importance can occur for

---

[4] Mitzvot are the 613 commandments found in the Torah that please God. There are positive and negative commandments. The list was first development by Maimonides. The full list can be found at: ttp://www.jewfaq.org/613.htm.

the names of places. The time it takes to travel between locations can supply insight into the event.

Keyphrases are identified in verses when they are essential to an understanding of that passage. There are no rules for selecting the keywords. Searching for other occurrences of the keywords in Scripture in a concordance is necessary to understand the word's usage; this must be done in either Hebrew or Greek, not in English. A classic Hebraic approach is to find the usage of a word in the Scripture by finding other verses that contain the word. The usage of a word, in its original language, is discovered by searching the Scripture in the language of the word. Verses that contain the word are identified, and a pattern for the usage of the word discovered. Each verse is examined to see what the usage of the word is which, may reveal a model for the word's usage. For Hebrew words the first usage of the word in the Scripture, primarily if used in the Torah, is essential. For the Greek words, the Christian Scriptures are used to determine the word usage in the Scripture. Sometimes finding the equivalent Greek word in the Septuagint then analyzing its usage in Hebrew can be very helpful.

The Rules of Hillel are used when applicable. Hillel was a Torah scholar who lived shortly before Yeshua's day. Hillel developed several rules for Torah students to interpret the Scriptures which refer to halachic Midrash. In several cases, these rules are helpful in the analysis of the Scripture.

The cultural implications from the period of the writing are done after the linguistic analysis is completed. The culture is crucial because it is not explicitly referenced in the biblical narratives as indicated earlier.

From the linguistic analysis and the cultural understanding, it is possible to obtain a deeper meaning of the Scripture beyond the literal meaning of the plain text. That is what the listeners of Yeshua's time were doing. They put the linguistics and the culture together without even having to contemplate it. They simply did it.

The analysis will lead to a set of findings explaining what the passage meant in Yeshua's day. Most of the time the Hebraic analysis leads to the desire for more in-depth analysis to fully understand what Yeshua was talking about or what was happening to Him. Whatever the result, a new more in-depth understanding of the Scripture is obtained.

The components of the Process of Discovery are:

Language

  Process of Discovery

    Linguistics Section

      Linguistic Structure

      Discussion

      Questioning the Passage

      Verse Comparison of citations or proof text

      Translation Inconsistencies

      Biblical Personalities

      Biblical Locations

      Phrase Study

Scripture cross-references

Linguistic Echoes

Rules of Hillel

Culture Section

Discussion

Questioning the passage

Cultural Echoes

Culture and Linguistics Section

Discussion

Midrash

Zohar

Thoughts

Reflections

Only the application sections are included in this document.

Abbreviations

Bibleworks V10[5] was used for the Scriptures used in this study guide. Below are the abbreviations used in the software.

Pentateuch	GEN	EXO	LEV	NUM	DEU
Historical & Poetic	JOS 1KI NEH ECC	JDG 2KI EST SOL	RUT 1CH JOB	1SA 2CH PSA	2SA EZR PRO
Prophets	ISA HOS MIC ZEC	JER JOE NAH MAL	LAM AMO HAB	EZE OBA ZEP	DAN JON HAG
Gospels	MAT	MAR	LUK	JOH	ACT
Paul	ROM PHI 2TI	1CO COL TIT	2CO 1TH PHM	GAL 2TH	EPH 1TI
Apostles	HEB 2JO	JAM 3JO	1PE JUD	2PE REV	1JO

---

[5] "Bible Version Abbreviations." *Abbreviations*. N.p., n.d. Web. 29 Oct. 2016.

Apocrypha	1ES	BAR	1MA	SIR	TBS
	3MA	PRM	WIS	BEL	SUT
	PSS	TOB	SUS	LAO	DAT
	PRA	OD	4ES	ESG	BET
	JDT	E	2MA	JSA	DN
	4MA	EPJ	SIP	JDA	G
		PSX			

The following is a list of aliases for BibleWorks book name abbreviations. See the <u>Book Names</u> section of the Options window for details on how to add to or change these aliases.

Internal Name	**Name used in Browse Window**	**Name used in Exported Verse Lists**	**Alias 1**	**Alias 2**
Gen	Genesis	Gen.	Gen	Genesis
Exo	Exodus	Exod.	Exo	Exodus
Lev	Leviticus	Lev.	Lev	Leviticus
Num	Numbers	Num.	Num	Numbers
Deu	Deuteronomy	Deut.	Deu	Deuteronomy
Jos	Joshua	Jos.	Jos	Joshua

Jdg	Judges	Jdg.	Jdg	Judges
Rut	Ruth	Ruth	Rut	Ruth
1Sa	1 Samuel	1 Sam.	1Sa	1Samuel
2Sa	2 Samuel	2 Sam.	2Sa	2Samuel
1Ki	1 Kings	1 Ki.	1Ki	1Kings
2Ki	2 Kings	2 Ki.	2Ki	2Kings
1Ch	1 Chronicles	1 Chr.	1Ch	1Chronicles
2Ch	2 Chronicles	2 Chr.	2Ch	2 Chronicles
Ezr	Ezra	Ezr.	Ezr	Ezra
Neh	Nehemiah	Neh.	Neh	Nehemiah
Est	Esther	Est.	Est	Esther
Job	Job	Job	Job	Job
Psa	Psalm	Ps.	Psa	Psalm
Pro	Proverbs	Prov.	Pro	Proverbs
Ecc	Ecclesiastes	Eccl.	Ecc	Ecclesiastes
Sol	Song of Solomon	Cant.	Sol	Song
Isa	Isaiah	Isa.	Isa	Isaiah
Jer	Jeremiah	Jer.	Jer	Jeremiah
Lam	Lamentations	Lam.	Lam	Lamentations
Eze	Ezekiel	Ezek.	Eze	Ezekiel
Dan	Daniel	Dan.	Dan	Daniel
Hos	Hosea	Hos.	Hos	Hosea

Joe	Joel	Joel	Joe	Joel
Amo	Amos	Amos	Amo	Amos
Oba	Obadiah	Obad.	Oba	Obadiah
Jon	Jonah	Jon.	Jon	Jonah
Mic	Micah	Mic.	Mic	Micah
Nah	Nahum	Nah.	Nah	Nahum
Hab	Habakkuk	Hab.	Hab	Habakkuk
Zep	Zephaniah	Zeph.	Zep	Zephaniah
Hag	Haggai	Hag.	Hag	Haggai
Zec	Zechariah	Zech.	Zec	Zechariah
Mal	Malachi	Mal.	Mal	Malachi
Mat	Matthew	Matt.	Mat	Matthew
Mar	Mark	Mk.	Mar	Mark
Luk	Luke	Lk.	Luk	Luke
Joh	John	Jn.	Joh	John
Act	Acts	Acts	Act	Acts
Rom	Romans	Rom.	Rom	Romans
1Co	1 Corinthians	1 Co.	1Co	1Corinthians
2Co	2 Corinthians	2 Co.	2Co	2Corinthians
Gal	Galatians	Gal.	Gal	Galatians
Eph	Ephesians	Eph.	Eph	Ephesians

Phi	Philippians	Phil.	Phi	Philippians
Col	Colossians	Col.	Col	Colossians
1Th	1 Thessaloni ans	1 Thess.	1Th	1Thessaloni ans
2Th	2 Thessaloni ans	2 Thess.	2Th	2Thessaloni ans
1Ti	1 Timothy	1 Tim.	1Ti	1Timothy
2Ti	2 Timothy	2 Tim.	2Ti	2Timothy
Tit	Titus	Tit.	Tit	Titus
Phm	Philemon	Phlm.	Ph m	Philemon
Heb	Hebrews	Heb.	Heb	Hebrews
Jam	James	Jas.	Jam	James
1Pe	1 Peter	1 Pet.	1Pe	1Peter
2Pe	2 Peter	2 Pet.	2Pe	2Peter
1Jo	1 John	1 Jn.	1Jo	1John
2Jo	2 John	2 Jn.	2Jo	2John
3Jo	3 John	3 Jn.	3Jo	3John
Jud	Jude	Jude	Jud	Jude
Rev	Revelation	Rev.	Rev	Revelation
1Es	1 Esdras	1 Es.	1Es	1Esdras
Jdt	Judith	Jdt.	Jdt	Judith
Tob	Tobit	Tob.	Tob	Tobit
1Ma	1 Maccabees	1 Ma.	1Ma	1Maccabees

2Ma	2 Maccabees	2 Ma.	2Ma	2Maccabees
3Ma	3 Maccabees	3 Ma.	3Ma	3Maccabees
4Ma	4 Maccabees	4 ma.	4Ma	4Maccabees
Ode	Odes	Odes	Ode	Odes
Wis	Wisdom	Wis.	Wis	Wisdom
Sir	Sirach	Sir.	Sir	Sirach
Sip	Sip	Sip	Sip	Sip
Pss	Psalms of Solomon	Ps. Sol.	Pss	
Bar	Baruch	Bar.	Bar	Baruch
Epj	Epistle of Jeremiah	Ep. Jer.	Epj	
Sus	Susanna	Sus.	Sus	Susanna
Bel	Bel	Bel.	Bel	Bel
Pra	Prayer of Azariah	Pr. Az.	Pra	Azariah
Dng	Daniel (Greek)	Dng	Dng	Dng
Prm	Prayer of Manasseh	Pr. Man.	Prm	Manasseh
Psx	Psalm(151)	Psx.	Psx	
Lao	Laodiceans	Lao.	Lao	Laodiceans
4Es	4 Esdras	4 Es.	4Es	4Esdras

Esg	Esther (Greek)	Esg.	Esg	
Jsa	Joshua (A)	Jsa.	Jsa	
Jda	Judges (A)	Jda.	Jda	
Tbs	Tobit (S)	Tbs.	Tbs	
Sut	Susanna (TH)	Sut.	Sut	
Dat	Daniel (TH)	Dat.	Dat	
Bet	Bel (TH)	Bet.	Bet	
WCF	WCF	WCF	WCF	
WLC	WLC	WLC	WLC	
WSC	WSC	WSC	WSC	

Chapter One

Language

New American Standard 1995	Hebrew
[1] Now it came about in the days when the judges governed, that there was a famine in the land. And a certain man of Bethlehem in Judah went to sojourn in the land of Moab with his wife and his two sons. [2] The name of the man *was* Elimelech, and the name of his wife, Naomi; and the names of his two sons *were* Mahlon and Chilion, Ephrathites of Bethlehem in Judah. Now they entered the land of Moab and remained there. [3] Then Elimelech, Naomi's husband, died; and she was left with her two sons. [4] They took for themselves Moabite women *as* wives; the name of the one was Orpah and the name of the other Ruth. And they lived there about ten years.	¹ וַיְהִ֗י בִּימֵי֙ שְׁפֹ֣ט הַשֹּׁפְטִ֔ים וַיְהִ֥י רָעָ֖ב בָּאָ֑רֶץ וַיֵּ֨לֶךְ אִ֜ישׁ מִבֵּ֧ית לֶ֣חֶם יְהוּדָ֗ה לָגוּר֙ בִּשְׂדֵ֣י מוֹאָ֔ב ה֥וּא וְאִשְׁתּ֖וֹ וּשְׁנֵ֥י בָנָֽיו: ² וְשֵׁ֣ם הָאִ֣ישׁ אֱלִימֶ֡לֶךְ וְשֵׁם֩ אִשְׁתּ֨וֹ נָעֳמִ֜י וְשֵׁ֥ם שְׁנֵֽי־בָנָ֣יו ׀ מַחְל֤וֹן וְכִלְיוֹן֙ אֶפְרָתִ֔ים מִבֵּ֥ית לֶ֖חֶם יְהוּדָ֑ה וַיָּבֹ֥אוּ שְׂדֵי־מוֹאָ֖ב וַיִּהְיוּ־שָֽׁם: ³ וַיָּ֥מָת אֱלִימֶ֖לֶךְ אִ֣ישׁ נָעֳמִ֑י וַתִּשָּׁאֵ֥ר הִ֖יא וּשְׁנֵ֥י בָנֶֽיהָ: ⁴ וַיִּשְׂא֣וּ לָהֶ֗ם נָשִׁים֙ מֹֽאֲבִיּ֔וֹת שֵׁ֤ם הָֽאַחַת֙ עָרְפָּ֔ה וְשֵׁ֥ם הַשֵּׁנִ֖ית ר֑וּת וַיֵּ֥שְׁבוּ שָׁ֖ם כְּעֶ֥שֶׂר שָׁנִֽים: ⁵ וַיָּמ֥וּתוּ גַם־שְׁנֵיהֶ֖ם מַחְל֣וֹן וְכִלְי֑וֹן וַתִּשָּׁאֵר֙ הָֽאִשָּׁ֔ה מִשְּׁנֵ֥י יְלָדֶ֖יהָ וּמֵאִישָֽׁהּ: ⁶ וַתָּ֤קָם הִיא֙ וְכַלֹּתֶ֔יהָ וַתָּ֖שָׁב מִשְּׂדֵ֣י מוֹאָ֑ב כִּ֤י שָֽׁמְעָה֙ בִּשְׂדֵ֣ה

5 Then both Mahlon and Chilion also died, and the woman was bereft of her two children and her husband.

6 Then she arose with her daughters-in-law that she might return from the land of Moab, for she had heard in the land of Moab that the LORD had visited His people in giving them food.

7 So she departed from the place where she was, and her two daughters-in-law with her; and they went on the way to return to the land of Judah.

8 And Naomi said to her two daughters-in-law, "Go, return each of you to her mother's house. May the LORD deal kindly with you as you have dealt with the dead and with me.

9 "May the LORD grant that you may find rest, each in the house of her husband." Then she kissed them, and they lifted up their voices and wept.

10 And they said to her, "*No,* but we will surely

מוֹאָב כִּי־פָקַד יְהוָה אֶת־עַמּוֹ לָתֵת לָהֶם לָחֶם:

7 וַתֵּצֵא מִן־הַמָּקוֹם אֲשֶׁר הָיְתָה־שָּׁמָּה וּשְׁתֵּי כַלֹּתֶיהָ עִמָּהּ וַתֵּלַכְנָה בַדֶּרֶךְ לָשׁוּב אֶל־אֶרֶץ יְהוּדָה:

8 וַתֹּאמֶר נָעֳמִי לִשְׁתֵּי כַלֹּתֶיהָ לֵכְנָה שֹּׁבְנָה אִשָּׁה לְבֵית אִמָּהּ (יַעֲשֶׂה) [יַעַשׂ] יְהוָה עִמָּכֶם חֶסֶד כַּאֲשֶׁר עֲשִׂיתֶם עִם־הַמֵּתִים וְעִמָּדִי:

9 יִתֵּן יְהוָה לָכֶם וּמְצֶאןָ מְנוּחָה אִשָּׁה בֵּית אִישָׁהּ וַתִּשַּׁק לָהֶן וַתִּשֶּׂאנָה קוֹלָן וַתִּבְכֶּינָה:

10 וַתֹּאמַרְנָה־לָּהּ כִּי־אִתָּךְ נָשׁוּב לְעַמֵּךְ:

11 וַתֹּאמֶר נָעֳמִי שֹׁבְנָה בְנֹתַי לָמָּה תֵלַכְנָה עִמִּי הַעוֹד־לִי בָנִים בְּמֵעַי וְהָיוּ לָכֶם לַאֲנָשִׁים:

12 שֹׁבְנָה בְנֹתַי לֵכְןָ כִּי זָקַנְתִּי מִהְיוֹת לְאִישׁ כִּי אָמַרְתִּי יֶשׁ־לִי תִקְוָה גַּם הָיִיתִי הַלַּיְלָה לְאִישׁ וְגַם יָלַדְתִּי בָנִים:

13 הֲלָהֵן תְּשַׂבֵּרְנָה עַד אֲשֶׁר יִגְדָּלוּ הֲלָהֵן תֵּעָגֵנָה לְבִלְתִּי הֱיוֹת לְאִישׁ אַל בְּנֹתַי כִּי־מַר

return with you to your people."

11 But Naomi said, "Return, my daughters. Why should you go with me? Have I yet sons in my womb, that they may be your husbands?

12 "Return, my daughters! Go, for I am too old to have a husband. If I said I have hope, if I should even have a husband tonight and also bear sons,

13 would you therefore wait until they were grown? Would you therefore refrain from marrying? No, my daughters; for it is harder for me than for you, for the hand of the LORD has gone forth against me."

14 And they lifted up their voices and wept again; and Orpah kissed her mother-in-law, but Ruth clung to her.

15 Then she said, "Behold, your sister-in-law has gone back to her people and her gods; return after your sister-in-law."

16 But Ruth said, "Do not urge me to leave you or turn back from following you;

לִי מְאֹד֙ מִכֶּ֔ם כִּֽי־יָצְאָ֥ה בִ֖י יַד־יְהוָֽה׃

14 וַתִּשֶּׂ֣נָה קוֹלָ֔ן וַתִּבְכֶּ֖ינָה ע֑וֹד וַתִּשַּׁ֤ק עָרְפָּה֙ לַחֲמוֹתָ֔הּ וְר֖וּת דָּ֥בְקָה בָּֽהּ׃

15 וַתֹּ֗אמֶר הִנֵּה֙ שָׁ֣בָה יְבִמְתֵּ֔ךְ אֶל־עַמָּ֖הּ וְאֶל־אֱלֹהֶ֑יהָ שׁ֖וּבִי אַחֲרֵ֥י יְבִמְתֵּֽךְ׃

16 וַתֹּ֤אמֶר רוּת֙ אַל־תִּפְגְּעִי־בִ֔י לְעָזְבֵ֖ךְ לָשׁ֣וּב מֵאַחֲרָ֑יִךְ כִּ֠י אֶל־אֲשֶׁ֨ר תֵּלְכִ֜י אֵלֵ֗ךְ וּבַאֲשֶׁ֤ר תָּלִ֙ינִי֙ אָלִ֔ין עַמֵּ֣ךְ עַמִּ֔י וֵאלֹהַ֖יִךְ אֱלֹהָֽי׃

17 בַּאֲשֶׁ֤ר תָּמ֙וּתִי֙ אָמ֔וּת וְשָׁ֖ם אֶקָּבֵ֑ר כֹּה֩ יַעֲשֶׂ֨ה יְהוָ֥ה לִי֙ וְכֹ֣ה יֹסִ֔יף כִּ֣י הַמָּ֔וֶת יַפְרִ֖יד בֵּינִ֥י וּבֵינֵֽךְ׃

18 וַתֵּ֕רֶא כִּֽי־מִתְאַמֶּ֥צֶת הִ֖יא לָלֶ֣כֶת אִתָּ֑הּ וַתֶּחְדַּ֖ל לְדַבֵּ֥ר אֵלֶֽיהָ׃

19 וַתֵּלַ֣כְנָה שְׁתֵּיהֶ֔ם עַד־בֹּאָ֖נָה בֵּ֣ית לָ֑חֶם וַיְהִ֞י כְּבֹאָ֣נָה בֵּ֣ית לֶ֗חֶם וַתֵּהֹ֤ם כָּל־הָעִיר֙ עֲלֵיהֶ֔ן וַתֹּאמַ֖רְנָה הֲזֹ֥את נָעֳמִֽי׃

20 וַתֹּ֣אמֶר אֲלֵיהֶ֔ן אַל־תִּקְרֶ֥אנָה לִ֖י נָעֳמִ֑י קְרֶ֤אןָ לִי֙ מָרָ֔א כִּי־הֵמַ֥ר שַׁדַּ֛י לִ֖י מְאֹֽד׃

21 אֲנִי֙ מְלֵאָ֣ה הָלַ֔כְתִּי וְרֵיקָ֖ם הֱשִׁיבַ֣נִי יְהוָ֑ה לָ֣מָּה תִקְרֶ֣אנָה

for where you go, I will go, and where you lodge, I will lodge. Your people *shall be* my people, and your God, my God.

¹⁷ "Where you die, I will die, and there I will be buried. Thus may the LORD do to me, and worse, if *anything but* death parts you and me."

¹⁸ When she saw that she was determined to go with her, she said no more to her.

¹⁹ So they both went until they came to Bethlehem. And when they had come to Bethlehem, all the city was stirred because of them, and the women said, "Is this Naomi?"

²⁰ She said to them, "Do not call me Naomi; call me Mara, for the Almighty has dealt very bitterly with me.

²¹ "I went out full, but the LORD has brought me back empty. Why do you call me Naomi, since the LORD has witnessed against me and the Almighty has afflicted me?"

לִי נָעֳמִי וַיהֹוָה עָנָה בִי וְשַׁדַּי הֵרַע לִי:

²² וַתָּשָׁב נָעֳמִי וְרוּת הַמּוֹאֲבִיָּה כַלָּתָהּ עִמָּהּ הַשָּׁבָה מִשְּׂדֵי מוֹאָב וְהֵמָּה בָּאוּ בֵּית לֶחֶם בִּתְחִלַּת קְצִיר שְׂעֹרִים:

[22] So Naomi returned, and with her Ruth the Moabitess, her daughter-in-law, who returned from the land of Moab. And they came to Bethlehem at the beginning of barley harvest.

Process of Discovery

Linguistics Section

Linguistic Structure

A [1] Now it came about in the days when the judges governed, that there was a famine in the land. And a certain man of Bethlehem in Judah went to sojourn in the land of Moab with his wife and his two sons. [2] The name of the man *was* Elimelech, and the name of his wife, Naomi; and the names of his two sons *were* Mahlon and Chilion, Ephrathites of Bethlehem in Judah. Now they entered the land of Moab and remained there.

> **B** [3] Then Elimelech, Naomi's husband, died; and she was left with her two sons.

A' [4] They took for themselves Moabite women *as* wives; the name of the one was Orpah and the name of the other Ruth. And they lived there about ten years.

> **B'** [5] Then both Mahlon and Chilion also died, and the woman was bereft of her two children and her husband.

A [6] Then she arose with her daughters-in-law that she might return from the land of Moab, for she had heard in the land of Moab that the LORD had visited His people in giving them food. [7] So she departed from the place where she was, and her two daughters-in-law with her; and they went on the way to return to the land of Judah. [8] And Naomi said to her two daughters-in-law, "Go, return each of you to her mother's house. May the LORD deal kindly with you as you have dealt with the dead and with me. [9] "May the LORD grant that you may find rest, each in the house of her husband." Then she kissed them, and they lifted up their voices and wept.

B ¹⁰ And they said to her, "*No*, but we will surely return with you to your people."

C ¹¹ But Naomi said, "Return, my daughters. Why should you go with me? Have I yet sons in my womb, that they may be your husbands? ¹² "Return, my daughters! Go, for I am too old to have a husband. If I said I have hope, if I should even have a husband tonight and also bear sons, ¹³ would you therefore wait until they were grown? Would you therefore refrain from marrying? No, my daughters; for it is harder for me than for you, for the hand of the LORD has gone forth against me."

D ¹⁴ And they lifted up their voices and wept again; and Orpah kissed her mother-in-law, but Ruth clung to her.

A' ¹⁵ Then she said, "Behold, your sister-in-law has gone back to her people and her gods; return after your sister-in-law."

B' ¹⁶ But Ruth said, "Do not urge me to leave you *or* turn back from following you; for where you go, I will go, and where you lodge, I will lodge. Your people *shall be* my people, and your God, my God. ¹⁷ "Where you die, I will die, and there I will be buried. Thus may the LORD do to me, and worse, if *anything but* death parts you and me." [18] When she saw that she was determined to go with her, she said no more to her.

> **C'** [19] So they both went until they came to Bethlehem. And when they had come to Bethlehem, all the city was stirred because of them, and the women said, "Is this Naomi?" [20] She said to them, "Do not call me Naomi; call me Mara, for the Almighty has dealt very bitterly with me. [21] "I went out full, but the LORD has brought me back empty. Why do you call me Naomi, since the LORD has witnessed against me and the Almighty has afflicted me?"

> **D'** [22] So Naomi returned, and with her Ruth the Moabitess, her daughter-in-law, who returned from the land of Moab. And they came to Bethlehem at the beginning of barley harvest.

Discussion

The story commences with Naomi, her husband, and her two sons traveling to Moab. In Moab, the two sons get married. Naomi's husband and two sons died in Moab. Naomi decided to go home to Bethlehem. Ruth decided to stay with her mother-in-law and traveled with her to Bethlehem.

Questioning the Passage[6]

1. When did Ruth live? (v. 1)

    Verse one says that the story of Ruth occurred during the time of the Judges.

---

[6] The questions and answers offered are for discussion purposes. You may have different questions and answers. Remember all questions are valid and all answers must be defendable from Scripture. This applies to this section and to the Culture Section.

2. Why did Naomi's two sons marry Moabite women? (v. 4)

The famine in Israel must have continued, which prevented Naomi and her sons from returning to the land. The two sons married Moabite women, which is forbidden.

> [3] "No Ammonite or Moabite shall enter the assembly of the LORD; none of their *descendants*, even to the tenth generation, shall ever enter the assembly of the LORD, (Deut. 23:3 NAU)

The Talmud says that Ruth and Oprah were daughters of Eglon, King of the Moabites. In the book of Judges, when Elgon met Ehud, a judge of Israel, he stood up when Ehud told him that the LORD had a message for him. Since Eglon showed respect to the LORD, the Talmud says that Eglon became a part of the line of King David. Therefore, the LORD permitted the sons to marry Moabite women.

3. Why did Naomi return to Israel? (v. 6)

Naomi heard that the LORD had visited Israel and ended the drought. The famine in the land of Israel was over. There was no need for Naomi to stay in Moab. Therefore, she prepared to go home.

4. Why did Naomi tell her daughters-in-law to go home opposed to returning to Israel with her? (v. 9)

Naomi did not want to return to Bethlehem with two Moabite daughters-in-law because she was embarrassed by them. Her sons decided to marry women who were an enemy of Israel.[7]

5. Why did Ruth insist on staying with Naomi? (v. 16)

The Zohar Cadash/Ibn Ezra says that this was a test Naomi set for Ruth.

Biblical Personalities

1. Elimelech was the husband of Naomi

2. Naomi was the wife of Elimelech

3. Mahlon was the son of Elimelech and Naomi

4. Chilion was the son of Elimelech and Naomi

---

[7] Meir Zlotowitz and Nosson Scherman, *The Five Megillos. a New Translation with a Commentary Anthologized from Talmudic, Midrashic and Rabbinic Sources* (Mesorah Publ., 1993).

Biblical Locations

1. Bethlehem, Moab (map shows Ruth's travels)

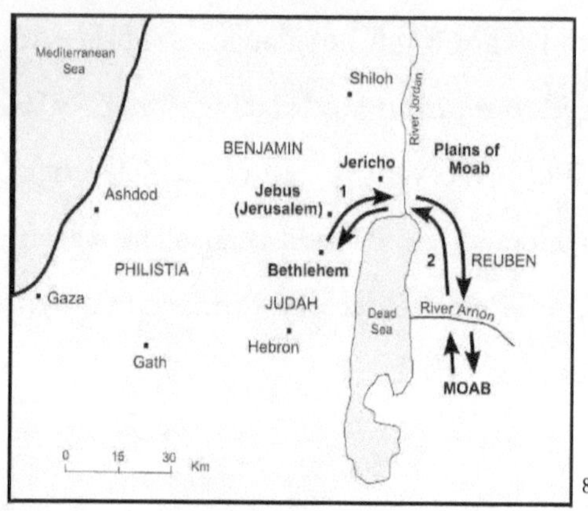

8

Phrase Study

1. לִי מָרָא כִּי־הֵמַר שַׁדַּי לִי מְאֹד

(Ruth 1:20 WTT)

Mara means bitterness. However, the word is spelled with an ending *aleph* instead of the usual *he*. This was done to accentuate the extent of her bitterness. This final letter substitution can be found in two other places in the Hebrew Scriptures, Numbers 11:20 and Daniel 11:44

---

[8] The Bible Journey | powered by Edit.com, "Ruth's Journey to Bethlehem," Header, accessed May 7, 2019, https://www.thebiblejourney.org/biblejourney2/29-the-journeys-of-ruth-and-samuel/ruths-journey-to-bethlehem/.

Culture Section

Discussion

During a time of famine and drought, enemies put aside, their differences and hospitality became the word of the day. The famine was severe in Israel during Ruth's time. The people of Moab saw what was happening in Israel and in their land, food was plentiful. Therefore, the Moabites freely opened their borders to any Israelite who wanted to cross. Israelites are the descendants of Abraham while the Moabites were the descendants of Lot. When Joshua conquered the land of Israel tension rose between the Moabites and Israelites.

Questioning the passage

1. Why did Naomi tell her daughters-in-law to return to the house of their husbands? (v. 9)

   How can the wives return to the house of their husbands when their husbands are dead? The Aramaic version of this verse says, "in the house of your parents." Near Eastern culture was that when a husband died, the widow would return to the house of her parents; in other words, she would return to live with her family.[9]

2. Does verses sixteen to eighteen indicates a religious conversion?

Ruth accepted the LORD because of the kindness and love that her mother-in-law showed her. Ruth must have seen the love of the LORD shining through Naomi. Naomi did not have an obligation to the daughters-in-law because she was not capable of having children. Ruth decided to abandon her Moabite home and gods to become a part of Israel and to worship the God of Israel.[10]

Midrash

The Midrash of Ruth says that when Naomi and Ruth entered Bethlehem that the entire city became tumultuous because of them. The Midrash explains that the news traveled quickly because it was a day for counting the Omer and the town people were together for the ceremony. The wife of Boaz died

---

[9] Rocco A. Errico and George M. Lamsa, *Aramaic Light on Joshua Through 2 Chronicles* (Smyma, GA: Noohra Foundation, 2009).
[10] IBID.

that day, and the people were also in prayer for the family.[11] The people did not know that they were meeting Boaz's future wife.

Zohar

In the Zohar Cadash/Ibn Ezra it is written that Ruth and Orpah had converted to Judaism when they married Naomi's two sons. Naomi was testing the resolve of their new faith when she told them to return to their people.[12] Naomi knew that the family would have a problem accepting the two women back once they learned that they had become Jews. Orpah was not dedicated to the LORD and elected to return to her family. Ruth was dedicated to the LORD and demonstrated her faith by telling Naomi that her place was with her mother-in-law in the land of Judah.

---

[11] IBID.

[12] Meir Zlotowitz and Nosson Scherman, *The Five Megillos. a New Translation with a Commentary Anthologized from Talmudic, Midrashic and Rabbinic Sources* (Mesorah Publ., 1993).

Thoughts

Ruth had taken the necessary oaths to convert to Judaism. When she was allowed to return to her family in Moab and go back to her old way of life and religion, she refused. This demonstrated her devotion to the LORD. Her sister, Orpah, was not dedicated to the LORD and converted to Judaism for her husband. Ruth's demonstration of her love for the LORD was rewarded by her becoming the great-great-grandmother of King David.

Reflections

How dedicated are you to the LORD? Ruth became devoted to the LORD and proved that even in tragedy. She did not lose her faith in the LORD. Randomness is a part of life's path. When the bad times come, one's faith in the LORD is tested. How would you do in the face of tragedy?

Chapter Two

Language

New American Standard 1995	Hebrew
¹ Now Naomi had a kinsman of her husband, a man of great wealth, of the family of Elimelech, whose name was Boaz. ² And Ruth the Moabitess said to Naomi, "Please let me go to the field and glean among the ears of grain after one in whose sight I may find favor." And she said to her, "Go, my daughter." ³ So she departed and went and gleaned in the field after the reapers; and she happened to come to the portion of the field belonging to Boaz, who was of the family of Elimelech. ⁴ Now behold, Boaz came from Bethlehem and said to the reapers, "May the LORD be with you." And they said to him, "May the LORD bless you."	¹ וּלְנָעֳמִי (מְיֻדָּע) [מוֹדַע] לְאִישָׁהּ אִישׁ גִּבּוֹר חַיִל מִמִּשְׁפַּחַת אֱלִימֶלֶךְ וּשְׁמוֹ בֹּעַז: ² וַתֹּאמֶר רוּת הַמּוֹאֲבִיָּה אֶל־נָעֳמִי אֵלְכָה־נָּא הַשָּׂדֶה וַאֲלַקֳטָה בַשִּׁבֳּלִים אַחַר אֲשֶׁר אֶמְצָא־חֵן בְּעֵינָיו וַתֹּאמֶר לָהּ לְכִי בִתִּי: ³ וַתֵּלֶךְ וַתָּבוֹא וַתְּלַקֵּט בַּשָּׂדֶה אַחֲרֵי הַקֹּצְרִים וַיִּקֶר מִקְרֶהָ חֶלְקַת הַשָּׂדֶה לְבֹעַז אֲשֶׁר מִמִּשְׁפַּחַת אֱלִימֶלֶךְ: ⁴ וְהִנֵּה־בֹעַז בָּא מִבֵּית לֶחֶם וַיֹּאמֶר לַקּוֹצְרִים יְהוָה עִמָּכֶם וַיֹּאמְרוּ לוֹ יְבָרֶכְךָ יְהוָה: ⁵ וַיֹּאמֶר בֹּעַז לְנַעֲרוֹ הַנִּצָּב עַל־הַקּוֹצְרִים לְמִי הַנַּעֲרָה הַזֹּאת:

5 Then Boaz said to his servant who was in charge of the reapers, "Whose young woman is this?"

6 The servant in charge of the reapers replied, "She is the young Moabite woman who returned with Naomi from the land of Moab.

7 "And she said, 'Please let me glean and gather after the reapers among the sheaves.' Thus she came and has remained from the morning until now; she has been sitting in the house for a little while."

8 Then Boaz said to Ruth, "Listen carefully, my daughter. Do not go to glean in another field; furthermore, do not go on from this one, but stay here with my maids.

9 "Let your eyes be on the field which they reap, and go after them. Indeed, I have commanded the servants not to touch you. When you are thirsty, go to the water jars and drink from what the servants draw."

10 Then she fell on her face, bowing to the ground and said to him, "Why have I found favor in your sight that

6 וַיַּעַן הַנַּעַר הַנִּצָּב עַל־הַקּוֹצְרִים וַיֹּאמַר נַעֲרָה מוֹאֲבִיָּה הִיא הַשָּׁבָה עִם־נָעֳמִי מִשְּׂדֵה מוֹאָב:

7 וַתֹּאמֶר אֲלַקֳטָה־נָּא וְאָסַפְתִּי בָעֳמָרִים אַחֲרֵי הַקּוֹצְרִים וַתָּבוֹא וַתַּעֲמוֹד מֵאָז הַבֹּקֶר וְעַד־עַתָּה זֶה שִׁבְתָּהּ הַבַּיִת מְעָט:

8 וַיֹּאמֶר בֹּעַז אֶל־רוּת הֲלוֹא שָׁמַעַתְּ בִּתִּי אַל־תֵּלְכִי לִלְקֹט בְּשָׂדֶה אַחֵר וְגַם לֹא תַעֲבוּרִי מִזֶּה וְכֹה תִדְבָּקִין עִם־נַעֲרֹתָי:

9 עֵינַיִךְ בַּשָּׂדֶה אֲשֶׁר־יִקְצֹרוּן וְהָלַכְתְּ אַחֲרֵיהֶן הֲלוֹא צִוִּיתִי אֶת־הַנְּעָרִים לְבִלְתִּי נָגְעֵךְ וְצָמִת וְהָלַכְתְּ אֶל־הַכֵּלִים וְשָׁתִית מֵאֲשֶׁר יִשְׁאֲבוּן הַנְּעָרִים:

10 וַתִּפֹּל עַל־פָּנֶיהָ וַתִּשְׁתַּחוּ אָרְצָה וַתֹּאמֶר אֵלָיו מַדּוּעַ מָצָאתִי חֵן בְּעֵינֶיךָ לְהַכִּירֵנִי וְאָנֹכִי נָכְרִיָּה:

11 וַיַּעַן בֹּעַז וַיֹּאמֶר לָהּ הֻגֵּד הֻגַּד לִי כֹּל אֲשֶׁר־

you should take notice of me, since I am a foreigner?"

11 Boaz replied to her, "All that you have done for your mother-in-law after the death of your husband has been fully reported to me, and how you left your father and your mother and the land of your birth, and came to a people that you did not previously know.

12 "May the LORD reward your work, and your wages be full from the LORD, the God of Israel, under whose wings you have come to seek refuge."

13 Then she said, "I have found favor in your sight, my lord, for you have comforted me and indeed have spoken kindly to your maidservant, though I am not like one of your maidservants."

14 At mealtime Boaz said to her, "Come here, that you may eat of the bread and dip your piece of bread in the vinegar." So she sat beside the reapers; and he served her roasted grain, and she ate and was satisfied and had some left.

עָשִׂית אֶת־חֲמוֹתֵךְ אַחֲרֵי
מוֹת אִישֵׁךְ וַתַּעַזְבִי אָבִיךְ
וְאִמֵּךְ וְאֶרֶץ מוֹלַדְתֵּךְ
וַתֵּלְכִי אֶל־עַם אֲשֶׁר לֹא־
יָדַעַתְּ תְּמוֹל שִׁלְשׁוֹם:
12 יְשַׁלֵּם יְהוָה פָּעֳלֵךְ וּתְהִי
מַשְׂכֻּרְתֵּךְ שְׁלֵמָה מֵעִם
יְהוָה אֱלֹהֵי יִשְׂרָאֵל אֲשֶׁר־
בָּאת לַחֲסוֹת תַּחַת־
כְּנָפָיו:
13 וַתֹּאמֶר אֶמְצָא־חֵן
בְּעֵינֶיךָ אֲדֹנִי כִּי נִחַמְתָּנִי
וְכִי דִבַּרְתָּ עַל־לֵב
שִׁפְחָתֶךָ וְאָנֹכִי לֹא אֶהְיֶה
כְּאַחַת שִׁפְחֹתֶיךָ:
14 וַיֹּאמֶר לָה בֹעַז לְעֵת
הָאֹכֶל גֹּשִׁי הֲלֹם וְאָכַלְתְּ
מִן־הַלֶּחֶם וְטָבַלְתְּ פִּתֵּךְ
בַּחֹמֶץ וַתֵּשֶׁב מִצַּד
הַקּוֹצְרִים וַיִּצְבָּט־לָהּ קָלִי
וַתֹּאכַל וַתִּשְׂבַּע וַתֹּתַר:
15 וַתָּקָם לְלַקֵּט וַיְצַו בֹּעַז
אֶת־נְעָרָיו לֵאמֹר גַּם בֵּין
הָעֳמָרִים תְּלַקֵּט וְלֹא
תַכְלִימוּהָ:
16 וְגַם שֹׁל־תָּשֹׁלּוּ לָהּ מִן־
הַצְּבָתִים וַעֲזַבְתֶּם וְלִקְּטָה
וְלֹא תִגְעֲרוּ־בָהּ:

15 When she rose to glean, Boaz commanded his servants, saying, "Let her glean even among the sheaves, and do not insult her.
16 "Also you shall purposely pull out for her *some grain* from the bundles and leave *it* that she may glean, and do not rebuke her."
17 So she gleaned in the field until evening. Then she beat out what she had gleaned, and it was about an ephah of barley.
18 She took *it* up and went into the city, and her mother-in-law saw what she had gleaned. She also took *it* out and gave Naomi what she had left after she was satisfied.
19 Her mother-in-law then said to her, "Where did you glean today and where did you work? May he who took notice of you be blessed." So she told her mother-in-law with whom she had worked and said, "The name of the man with whom I worked today is Boaz."
20 Naomi said to her daughter-in-law, "May he be blessed of the LORD who

17 וַתְּלַקֵּט בַּשָּׂדֶה עַד־הָעָרֶב וַתַּחְבֹּט אֵת אֲשֶׁר־לִקֵּטָה וַיְהִי כְּאֵיפָה שְׂעֹרִים:
18 וַתִּשָּׂא וַתָּבוֹא הָעִיר וַתֵּרֶא חֲמוֹתָהּ אֵת אֲשֶׁר־לִקֵּטָה וַתּוֹצֵא וַתִּתֶּן־לָהּ אֵת אֲשֶׁר־הוֹתִרָה מִשָּׂבְעָהּ:
19 וַתֹּאמֶר לָהּ חֲמוֹתָהּ אֵיפֹה לִקַּטְתְּ הַיּוֹם וְאָנָה עָשִׂית יְהִי מַכִּירֵךְ בָּרוּךְ וַתַּגֵּד לַחֲמוֹתָהּ אֵת אֲשֶׁר־עָשְׂתָה עִמּוֹ וַתֹּאמֶר שֵׁם הָאִישׁ אֲשֶׁר עָשִׂיתִי עִמּוֹ הַיּוֹם בֹּעַז:
20 וַתֹּאמֶר נָעֳמִי לְכַלָּתָהּ בָּרוּךְ הוּא לַיהוָה אֲשֶׁר לֹא־עָזַב חַסְדּוֹ אֶת־הַחַיִּים וְאֶת־הַמֵּתִים וַתֹּאמֶר לָהּ נָעֳמִי קָרוֹב לָנוּ הָאִישׁ מִגֹּאֲלֵנוּ הוּא:
21 וַתֹּאמֶר רוּת הַמּוֹאֲבִיָּה גַּם כִּי־אָמַר אֵלַי עִם־הַנְּעָרִים אֲשֶׁר־לִי תִּדְבָּקִין עַד אִם־כִּלּוּ אֵת כָּל־הַקָּצִיר אֲשֶׁר־לִי:

has not withdrawn his kindness to the living and to the dead." Again Naomi said to her, "The man is our relative, he is one of our closest relatives."

²¹ Then Ruth the Moabitess said, "Furthermore, he said to me, 'You should stay close to my servants until they have finished all my harvest.'"

²² Naomi said to Ruth her daughter-in-law, "It is good, my daughter, that you go out with his maids, so that *others* do not fall upon you in another field."

²³ So she stayed close by the maids of Boaz in order to glean until the end of the barley harvest and the wheat harvest. And she lived with her mother-in-law.

²² וַתֹּאמֶר נָעֳמִי אֶל־רוּת כַּלָּתָהּ טוֹב בִּתִּי כִּי תֵצְאִי עִם־נַעֲרוֹתָיו וְלֹא יִפְגְּעוּ־בָךְ בְּשָׂדֶה אַחֵר: ²³ וַתִּדְבַּק בְּנַעֲרוֹת בֹּעַז לְלַקֵּט עַד־כְּלוֹת קְצִיר־הַשְּׂעֹרִים וּקְצִיר הַחִטִּים וַתֵּשֶׁב אֶת־חֲמוֹתָהּ:

Process of Discovery

Linguistics Section

Linguistic Structure

A [1] Now Naomi had a kinsman of her husband, a man of great wealth, of the family of Elimelech, whose name was Boaz. [2] And Ruth the Moabitess said to Naomi, "Please let me go to the field and glean among the ears of grain after one in whose sight I may find favor." And she said to her, "Go, my daughter."

B [3] So she departed and went and gleaned in the field after the reapers; and she happened to come to the portion of the field belonging to Boaz, who was of the family of Elimelech.

C [4] Now behold, Boaz came from Bethlehem and said to the reapers, "May the LORD be with you." And they said to him, "May the LORD bless you." [5] Then Boaz said to his servant who was in charge of the reapers, "Whose young woman is this?" [6] The servant in charge of the reapers replied, "She is the young Moabite woman who returned with Naomi from the land of Moab. [7] "And she said, 'Please let me glean and gather after the reapers among the sheaves.' Thus she came and has remained from the morning until now; she has been sitting in the house for a little while."

D [8] Then Boaz said to Ruth, "Listen carefully, my daughter. Do not go to glean in another field; furthermore, do not go on from this one, but stay here with my maids. [9] "Let your eyes be on the field which they reap, and go after them. Indeed, I have commanded the servants not to touch you. When you are thirsty, go to the water jars and drink from what the servants draw."

E [10] Then she fell on her face, bowing to the ground and said to him, "Why have I found favor in your sight that you should take notice of me, since I am a foreigner?"

F [11] Boaz replied to her, "All that you have done for your mother-in-law after the death of your husband has been fully reported to me, and how you left your father and your mother and the land of your birth, and came to a people that you did not previously know. [12] "May the LORD reward your work, and your wages be full from the LORD, the God of Israel, under whose wings you have come to seek refuge."

E' [13] Then she said, "I have found favor in your sight, my lord, for you have comforted me and indeed have spoken kindly to your maidservant, though I am not like one of your maidservants."

D' [14] At mealtime Boaz said to her, "Come here, that you may eat of the bread and dip your piece of bread in the vinegar." So she sat beside the reapers; and he served her roasted grain, and she ate and was satisfied and had some left.

C' [15] When she rose to glean, Boaz commanded his servants, saying, "Let her glean even among the sheaves, and do not insult her. [16] "Also you shall purposely pull out for her *some grain* from the bundles and leave *it* that she may glean, and do not rebuke her."

B' [17] So she gleaned in the field until evening. Then she beat out what she had gleaned, and it was about an ephah of barley.

A' [18] She took *it* up and went into the city, and her mother-in-law saw what she had gleaned. She also took *it* out and gave Naomi what she had left after she was satisfied. [19] Her mother-in-law then said to her, "Where did you glean today and where did you work? May he who took notice of you be blessed." So she told her mother-in-law with whom she had worked and said, "The name of the man with whom I worked today is Boaz." [20] Naomi said to her daughter-in-law, "May he be blessed of the LORD who has not withdrawn his kindness to the living and to the dead." Again Naomi said to her, "The man is our relative, he is one of our closest relatives." [21] Then Ruth the Moabitess said, "Furthermore, he said to me, 'You should stay close to my servants until they have finished all my harvest.'" [22] Naomi said to Ruth her daughter-in-law, "It is good, my daughter, that you go out with his maids, so that *others* do not fall upon you in another field." [23] So she stayed close by the maids of Boaz in order to glean until the end of the barley harvest and the wheat harvest. And she lived with her mother-in-law.

Discussion

The chapter is a very complicated chiasm. The center of the chiasm is when Boaz recognizes the righteous acts that Ruth performed for her other-in-law.

Questioning the Passage

1. Why does verse four begin with the word "behold?" The word "behold" informs the reader that something unusual was about to happen. It was not customary for Boaz to go out to his fields. The LORD must have provoked Boaz to go to his fields that day so that he could meet Ruth.[13]

2. Why did Boaz ask who Ruth was? (v. 5 & 6) Boaz asked this question because he had felt an attraction to Ruth. He wanted to know if she was a Hebrew. The Targum adds the words "and became a proselyte." This phrase indicates that even though Ruth was a Moabite, she had converted to the Hebrews'

---

[13] Meir Zlotowitz and Nosson Scherman, *The Five Megillos. a New Translation with a Commentary Anthologized from Talmudic, Midrashic and Rabbinic Sources* (Mesorah Publ., 1993).

religion. Therefore, when Boaz married Ruth, he did not violate the Torah, which told the people of Israel not to marry Moabite women.[14]

3. Why did Ruth ask permission to glean the field? (v. 3)

    The gleaning of the field was a right given to the poor by the Torah. Therefore, there was no reason to ask for permission to glean. Ruth asked for permission. By asking permission, Ruth demonstrated her good manners and respect for the culture of Israel.

4. Why did Boaz want Ruth to stay on his field, telling his servant to watch her? (v. 9)

    Boaz recognized Ruth as having a generous heart, and she was a righteous woman. Boaz knew that if a righteous woman was gleaning his fields, she would be a blessing.[15]

5. Why did Ruth fall upon her face? (v. 10)

---

[14] Derek Robert George. Beattie and J. Stanley. McIvor, *The Aramaic Bible* (T & T Clark, 1994).
[15] IBID.

Ruth was bowing down to Boaz, which was a sign of humility and acknowledging that he owned the field and that her existence was because of his generosity.

6. Why does verse twenty-one call Ruth the Moabitess? This is a reminder to the reader that Ruth was not from Israel but because of her kindness to her mother-in-law Naomi, and her conversion to the Jewish religion, that the LORD blessed her.

Translation Inconsistencies

1. ^{WTT} Ruth 2:1 וּלְנָעֳמִי (מְיֻדָּע) [מוֹדַע] לְאִישָׁהּ אִישׁ גִּבּוֹר חַיִל מִמִּשְׁפַּחַת אֱלִימֶלֶךְ וּשְׁמוֹ בֹּעַז׃

^{NAU} **Ruth 2:1** Now Naomi had a kinsman of her husband, a man of great wealth, of the family of Elimelech, whose name was Boaz.

^{NIV} **Ruth 2:1** Now Naomi had a relative on her husband's side, a man of standing from the clan of Elimelek, whose name was Boaz.

^{NRS} **Ruth 2:1** Now Naomi had a kinsman on her husband's side, a prominent rich man, of the family of Elimelech, whose name was Boaz.

^{NAS} **Ruth 2:1** Now Naomi had a kinsman of her husband, a man of great wealth, of the family of Elimelech, whose name was Boaz.

^TNK **Ruth 2:1** Now Naomi had a kinsman on her husband's side, a man of substance, of the family of Elimelech, whose name was Boaz.

The translation of "a man of great wealth" and "a great man of substance" are both possible translations. When examining the meaning of each verse, then compared to the rest of the story, the translation "a great man of substance" is a better translation.

Biblical Personalities

1. Boaz – "Boaz was a very wealthy man who lived in Bethlehem. When Naomi returned to Bethlehem with her widowed daughter-in-law, Ruth, Ruth went into the fields of Boaz to glean. Boaz learned that Ruth's deceased husband was a distant relative of his. He acted kindly towards Ruth and instructed his farm workers to leave extra sheaves of barley for her to gather. Ruth had another relative of her late husband, who was closer than Boaz. By law, the other relative was obligated to marry Ruth, as stated in Deuteronomy 25:5-10. Boaz confronted the other relative with this law, and after the relative refused

to marry Ruth, Boaz agreed to marry Ruth, and to buy the estate of Ruth's deceased husband."[16]

Phrase Study

1. אִישׁ גִּבּוֹר חַיִל

"A mighty man of substance" follows the Sage Rashi's[i] translation of a similar phrase in Exodus 18:21. This translation is a better fit for the rest of the story. Boaz was a man of substance not only allowing Ruth to glean his fields, but he also told his workers to leave some harvested grain behind. Boaz will continue to show his ethics by giving his distant cousin Naomi and Ruth the help they needed.

2. וְלֹא תַכְלִימוּהָ

This phrase translates best as "not to embarrass." Most of the English translations use the phrase "not to insult." Boaz did not want Ruth to feel embarrassed that she had to glean the fields to eat. He did not want any of his servants to insult her in any way that would embarrass her.

---

16 Boaz (or Booz), accessed May 10, 2019, http://www.aboutbibleprophecy.com/p153.htm.

Culture Section

Discussion

Gleaning was very common in Ruth's day. The reapers would go into the field for the harvest. Whatever was left and whatever fell from their hands was left for the women who did the gleaning. This was a form of charity for the poor. Food was scarce, and if a person was poor, they would go days without food. The poor would glean the fields.

Questioning the passage

1. What was roasted grain? (v. 14)

A custom in the Near East was to take ripened grain, salt it, place it on a fire until it split open, and then they would eat it. This expression is often confused with roasted corn. Corn was not known to the Near East until after the discovery of the Americas.[17]

---

[17] Rocco A. Errico and George M. Lamsa, *Aramaic Light on Joshua Through 2 Chronicles* (Smyma, GA: Noohra Foundation, 2009).

Thoughts

Random acts of kindness always have a "payoff." In the case of Ruth, her kindness to her mother-in-law Naomi translated into an unexpected win. Boaz took an interest in her because the righteousness that Ruth showed. Not only did she help her mother-in-law, which she was not obligated to do, but she also asked for permission to glean the fields, again something that she did not have to do. The world would be a better place if all of its inhabitants lived by the idea of showing kindness.

Reflections

In our society, which does not like to give compliments, it is difficult to perform acts of kindness. Too many people feel that they must get something in return for their kindness. It reminds me of when I got married. My mother insisted that all the presents be opened in front of her right after the reception so that she could make a list of the giver and the amount of money given, or the value of the gift. She used that list to ensure that she gave identically valued gifts. Her methodology had nothing to do with kindness but rather self-centeredness. Boaz gave to Ruth without expecting anything in return. That is why he was righteous, and my mother was not.

Chapter Three

Language

New American Standard 1995	Hebrew
1 Then Naomi her mother-in-law said to her, "My daughter, shall I not seek security for you, that it may be well with you? 2 "Now is not Boaz our kinsman, with whose maids you were? Behold, he winnows barley at the threshing floor tonight. 3 "Wash yourself therefore, and anoint yourself and put on your *best* clothes, and go down to the threshing floor; *but* do not make yourself known to the man until he has finished eating and drinking. 4 "It shall be when he lies down, that you shall notice the place where he lies, and you shall go and uncover his feet and lie down; then he will tell you what you shall do." 5 She said to her, "All that you say I will do."	1 וַתֹּאמֶר לָהּ נָעֳמִי חֲמוֹתָהּ בִּתִּי הֲלֹא אֲבַקֶּשׁ־לָךְ מָנוֹחַ אֲשֶׁר יִיטַב־לָךְ: 2 וְעַתָּה הֲלֹא בֹעַז מֹדַעְתָּנוּ אֲשֶׁר הָיִית אֶת־נַעֲרוֹתָיו הִנֵּה־הוּא זֹרֶה אֶת־גֹּרֶן הַשְּׂעֹרִים הַלָּיְלָה: 3 וְרָחַצְתְּ וָסַכְתְּ וְשַׂמְתְּ (שִׂמְלֹתֵךְ) [שִׂמְלֹתַיִךְ] עָלַיִךְ (וְיָרַדְתִּי) [וְיָרַדְתְּ] הַגֹּרֶן אַל־תִּוָּדְעִי לָאִישׁ עַד כַּלֹּתוֹ לֶאֱכֹל וְלִשְׁתּוֹת: 4 וִיהִי בְשָׁכְבוֹ וְיָדַעַתְּ אֶת־הַמָּקוֹם אֲשֶׁר יִשְׁכַּב־שָׁם וּבָאת וְגִלִּית מַרְגְּלֹתָיו (וְשָׁכָבְתִּי) [וְשָׁכָבְתְּ] וְהוּא יַגִּיד לָךְ אֵת אֲשֶׁר תַּעֲשִׂין: 5 וַתֹּאמֶר אֵלֶיהָ כֹּל אֲשֶׁר־תֹּאמְרִי (כר) [אֵלַי] אֶעֱשֶׂה: 6 וַתֵּרֶד הַגֹּרֶן וַתַּעַשׂ כְּכֹל אֲשֶׁר־צִוַּתָּה חֲמוֹתָהּ: 7 וַיֹּאכַל בֹּעַז וַיֵּשְׁתְּ וַיִּיטַב לִבּוֹ וַיָּבֹא לִשְׁכַּב בִּקְצֵה הָעֲרֵמָה וַתָּבֹא בַלָּט וַתְּגַל מַרְגְּלֹתָיו וַתִּשְׁכָּב:

⁶ So she went down to the threshing floor and did according to all that her mother-in-law had commanded her.

⁷ When Boaz had eaten and drunk and his heart was merry, he went to lie down at the end of the heap of grain; and she came secretly, and uncovered his feet and lay down.

⁸ It happened in the middle of the night that the man was startled and bent forward; and behold, a woman was lying at his feet.

⁹ He said, "Who are you?" And she answered, "I am Ruth your maid. So spread your covering over your maid, for you are a close relative."

¹⁰ Then he said, "May you be blessed of the LORD, my daughter. You have shown your last kindness to be better than the first by not going after young men, whether poor or rich.

¹¹ "Now, my daughter, do not fear. I will do for you whatever you ask, for all my people in the city know that

וַיְהִי בַּחֲצִי הַלַּיְלָה וַיֶּחֱרַד הָאִישׁ וַיִּלָּפֵת וְהִנֵּה אִשָּׁה שֹׁכֶבֶת מַרְגְּלֹתָיו: ⁸

וַיֹּאמֶר מִי־אָתְּ וַתֹּאמֶר אָנֹכִי רוּת אֲמָתֶךָ וּפָרַשְׂתָּ כְנָפֶךָ עַל־אֲמָתְךָ כִּי גֹאֵל אָתָּה: ⁹

וַיֹּאמֶר בְּרוּכָה אַתְּ לַיהוָה בִּתִּי הֵיטַבְתְּ חַסְדֵּךְ הָאַחֲרוֹן מִן־הָרִאשׁוֹן לְבִלְתִּי־לֶכֶת אַחֲרֵי הַבַּחוּרִים אִם־דַּל וְאִם־עָשִׁיר: ¹⁰

וְעַתָּה בִּתִּי אַל־תִּירְאִי כֹּל אֲשֶׁר־תֹּאמְרִי אֶעֱשֶׂה־לָּךְ כִּי יוֹדֵעַ כָּל־שַׁעַר עַמִּי כִּי אֵשֶׁת חַיִל אָתְּ: ¹¹

וְעַתָּה כִּי אָמְנָם כִּי (אם) [קק] גֹאֵל אָנֹכִי וְגַם יֵשׁ גֹּאֵל קָרוֹב מִמֶּנִּי: ¹²

לִינִי הַלַּיְלָה וְהָיָה בַבֹּקֶר אִם־יִגְאָלֵךְ טוֹב יִגְאָל וְאִם־לֹא יַחְפֹּץ לְגָאֳלֵךְ וּגְאַלְתִּיךְ אָנֹכִי חַי־יְהוָה שִׁכְבִי עַד־הַבֹּקֶר: ¹³

וַתִּשְׁכַּב (מרגלתו) [מַרְגְּלוֹתָיו] עַד־הַבֹּקֶר וַתָּקָם (בטרום) [בְּטֶרֶם] יַכִּיר אִישׁ אֶת־רֵעֵהוּ וַיֹּאמֶר אַל־יִוָּדַע כִּי־בָאָה הָאִשָּׁה הַגֹּרֶן: ¹⁴

וַיֹּאמֶר הָבִי הַמִּטְפַּחַת אֲשֶׁר־עָלַיִךְ וְאֶחֳזִי־בָהּ וַתֹּאחֶז בָּהּ וַיָּמָד שֵׁשׁ־שְׂעֹרִים וַיָּשֶׁת עָלֶיהָ וַיָּבֹא הָעִיר: ¹⁵

וַתָּבוֹא אֶל־חֲמוֹתָהּ וַתֹּאמֶר מִי־אַתְּ בִּתִּי וַתַּגֶּד־לָהּ אֵת כָּל־אֲשֶׁר עָשָׂה־לָהּ הָאִישׁ: ¹⁶

you are a woman of excellence.

12 "Now it is true I am a close relative; however, there is a relative closer than I.

13 "Remain this night, and when morning comes, if he will redeem you, good; let him redeem you. But if he does not wish to redeem you, then I will redeem you, as the LORD lives. Lie down until morning."

14 So she lay at his feet until morning and rose before one could recognize another; and he said, "Let it not be known that the woman came to the threshing floor."

15 Again he said, "Give me the cloak that is on you and hold it." So she held it, and he measured six *measures* of barley and laid *it* on her. Then she went into the city.

16 When she came to her mother-in-law, she said, "How did it go, my daughter?" And she told her all that the man had done for her.

17 She said, "These six *measures* of barley he gave to me, for he said, 'Do not go to

17 וַתֹּאמֶר שֵׁשׁ־הַשְּׂעֹרִים הָאֵלֶּה נָתַן לִי כִּי אָמַר (כר) [אֵלַי] אַל־תָּבוֹאִי רֵיקָם אֶל־חֲמוֹתֵךְ׃

18 וַתֹּאמֶר שְׁבִי בִתִּי עַד אֲשֶׁר תֵּדְעִין אֵיךְ יִפֹּל דָּבָר כִּי לֹא יִשְׁקֹט הָאִישׁ כִּי־אִם־כִּלָּה הַדָּבָר הַיּוֹם׃

<table>
<tr><td>

your mother-in-law empty-handed.'"

[18] Then she said, "Wait, my daughter, until you know how the matter turns out; for the man will not rest until he has settled it today."

</td><td></td></tr>
</table>

Process of Discovery

Linguistics Section

Linguistic Structure

[1] Then Naomi her mother-in-law said to her, "My daughter, shall I not seek security for you, that it may be well with you?

[Naomi's Instructions] [2] "Now is not Boaz our kinsman, with whose maids you were? Behold, he winnows barley at the threshing floor tonight. [3] "Wash yourself therefore, and anoint yourself and put on your *best* clothes, and go down to the threshing floor; *but* do not make yourself known to the man until he has finished eating and drinking. [4] "It shall be when he lies down, that you shall notice the place where he lies, and you shall go and uncover his feet and lie down; then he will tell you what you shall do."

[Ruth's Response] [5] She said to her, "All that you say I will do." [6] So she went down to the threshing floor and did according to all that her mother-in-law had commanded her. [7] When Boaz had eaten and drunk and his heart was merry, he went to lie down at the end of the heap of grain; and she came secretly, and uncovered his feet and lay down.

[The Action] [8] It happened in the middle of the night that the man was startled and bent forward; and behold, a woman was lying at his feet. [9] He said, "Who are you?" And she answered, "I am Ruth your maid. So spread your covering over your maid, for you are a close relative." [10] Then he said, "May you be blessed of the LORD, my daughter. You have shown your last kindness to be better than the first by not going after young men, whether poor or rich. [11] "Now, my daughter, do not fear. I will do for you whatever you ask, for all my people in the city know that you are a woman of excellence. [12] "Now it is true I am a close relative; however, there is a relative closer than I. [13] "Remain this night, and when morning comes, if he will redeem you, good; let him redeem you. But if he does not wish to redeem you, then I will redeem you, as the LORD lives. Lie down until morning."

[Morning] [14] So she lay at his feet until morning and rose before one could recognize another; and he said, "Let it not be known that the woman came to the threshing floor." [15] Again he said, "Give me the cloak that is on you and hold it." So she held it, and he measured six *measures* of barley and laid *it* on her. Then she went into the city.

[Ruth returns to Naomi] [16] When she came to her mother-in-law, she said, "How did it go, my daughter?" And she told her all that the man had done for her. [17] She said, "These six *measures* of barley he gave to me, for he said, 'Do not go to your mother-in-law empty-handed.'" [18] Then she said, "Wait, my daughter, until you know how the matter turns out; for the man will not rest until he has settled it today."

Discussion

This chapter discusses the events that occurred when Ruth made herself known to Boaz. The usual interpretation for this chapter is what was Ruth doing at the "foot" of Boaz. The word "foot" is a euphemism for the male sex organ and uncovering his feet can be interpreted as Ruth's lying at his "foot" has led to this conclusion. The narrative says that Boaz was pleased when he discovered Ruth at his foot.

Questioning the Passage

1. What does it mean that Boaz should redeem Ruth? (v. 13)

   If Boaz took Ruth to be his wife after the night they were together; then Ruth would have been considered redeemed. She would have a place to live. Naomi told Ruth that if she were not redeemed, then Naomi would continue to find a husband for Ruth.

2. Why did Boaz give Ruth six measures of barley? (v. 15)

   Boaz was grateful for Ruth staying with him through the night. He also knew that Ruth was a relative through Naomi. Boaz gave Ruth the grain because he wanted to help out a family member. It is a mitzvah to give to the poor.

3. What does it mean to wait to see how things turn out? (v. 18)

   Naomi told Ruth to wait and see if Boaz asks her to marry him.

Translation Inconsistencies

1. **Ruth 3:1** ^{WTT} וַתֹּאמֶר לָהּ נָעֳמִי חֲמוֹתָהּ בִּתִּי הֲלֹא אֲבַקֶּשׁ־לָךְ מָנוֹחַ אֲשֶׁר יִיטַב־לָךְ׃

^{NAU} **Ruth 3:1** Then Naomi her mother-in-law said to her, "My daughter, shall I not seek security for you, that it may be well with you?

^{NIV} **Ruth 3:1** One day Ruth's mother-in-law Naomi said to her, "My daughter, I must find a home for you, where you will be well provided for.

^{NRS} **Ruth 3:1** Naomi her mother-in-law said to her, "My daughter, I need to seek some security for you, so that it may be well with you.

^{CJB} **Ruth 3:1** Na'omi her mother-in-law said to her, "My daughter, I should be seeking security for you; so that things will go well with you.

^{KJV} **Ruth 3:1** Then Naomi her mother in law said unto her, My daughter, shall I not seek rest for thee, that it may be well with thee?

^{TNK} **Ruth 3:1** Naomi, her mother-in-law, said to her, "Daughter, I must seek a home for you, where you may be happy.

The inconsistency is "shall I not seek security for you." The Hebrew phrase *la* which is translated as "no" in several English versions but not in all is the issue. Naomi felt the obligation to find security for Ruth. In those days, that meant that Naomi needed to find a husband for Ruth. It was the men who cared for the women. Naomi did not have a third son for Ruth to marry. Customs of the day dictated that if a brother died without a child, then he was obligated to marry the widow. Therefore, Naomi felt obligated to find a husband for her daughter-in-law.

Culture Section

Discussion

Courtships between men and women did not occur in ancient times. Men and women rarely interacted with each other. Marriages were arranged using professional matchmakers. Marriages were arranged between the parents of the bride and groom.

Questioning the passage

1. Why did Boaz sleep on the threshing floor? (v. 3)

   During harvest time, the owner of a field would sleep on the threshing floor to protect his wheat. Wheat was scarce and was very valuable. A bed of straw or wheat was used for sleep.[18]

---

[18] Rocco A. Errico and George M. Lamsa, *Aramaic Light on Joshua Through 2 Chronicles* (Smyma, GA: Noohra Foundation, 2009).

2. What does it mean to uncover and lay at his feet?

Since the phrase "uncovered his feet" is in the Hebrew text, the Rabbis interpreted that Ruth was performing a sexual act. The reason for this is because in other places in the Scripture, the phrase "uncovering her nakedness" means to have sexual relations. This interpretation explains why Boaz was happy to see Ruth when the culture of the day demanded that women and men sleep in separate areas (except for a married couple). It is possible that Ruth did uncover Boaz's feet and laid there. Boaz's covering would have reached his feet.

The Targum says that Boaz had the desire to take Ruth but resisted in the same manner that Joseph did when he was approached in Egypt. It would not have been ethical for Boaz to take Ruth.

Thoughts

Courage! Ruth was courageous because she laid at Boaz's feet. The custom of the day kept men and women separated. To cross that cultural line was very difficult to do. Therefore, it shows that Ruth had courage. It is possible to say that since Ruth was a Moabite that the custom of men and women being separate was unknown to her. Ruth had to catch Boaz's attention, and she did that. Ruth was a widow and needed a husband. Her livelihood and survival depended upon that. So, Ruth gathered the courage to go to Boaz.

Chapter Four

Language

New American Standard 1995	Hebrew
[1] Now Boaz went up to the gate and sat down there, and behold, the close relative of whom Boaz spoke was passing by, so he said, "Turn aside, friend, sit down here." And he turned aside and sat down. [2] He took ten men of the elders of the city and said, "Sit down here." So they sat down. [3] Then he said to the closest relative, "Naomi, who has come back from the land of Moab, has to sell the piece of land which belonged to our brother Elimelech. [4] "So I thought to inform you, saying, 'Buy *it* before those who are sitting *here*, and before the elders of my people. If you will redeem *it*, redeem *it*; but if not, tell me that I may know; for there is	‎1 וּבֹעַז עָלָה הַשַּׁעַר֙ וַיֵּשֶׁב שָׁם֒ וְהִנֵּה הַגֹּאֵל עֹבֵר֙ אֲשֶׁר דִּבֶּר־בֹּעַז וַיֹּאמֶר סוּרָה שְׁבָה־פֹּה פְּלֹנִי אַלְמֹנִי וַיָּסַר וַיֵּשֵׁב: ‎2 וַיִּקַּח עֲשָׂרָה אֲנָשִׁים מִזִּקְנֵי הָעִיר וַיֹּאמֶר שְׁבוּ־פֹה וַיֵּשֵׁבוּ: ‎3 וַיֹּאמֶר֙ לַגֹּאֵל חֶלְקַת֙ הַשָּׂדֶה אֲשֶׁר לְאָחִינוּ לֶאֱלִימֶלֶךְ מָכְרָה נָעֳמִי הַשָּׁבָה מִשְּׂדֵה מוֹאָב: ‎4 וַאֲנִי אָמַרְתִּי אֶגְלֶה אָזְנְךָ לֵאמֹר קְנֵה נֶגֶד הַיֹּשְׁבִים֙ וְנֶגֶד זִקְנֵי עַמִּי֙ אִם־תִּגְאַל֙ גְּאָל וְאִם־לֹא יִגְאַל הַגִּידָה לִּי (וְאֵדַע) [וְאֵדְעָה֙] כִּי אֵין זוּלָתְךָ֙ לִגְאוֹל וְאָנֹכִי אַחֲרֶיךָ וַיֹּאמֶר אָנֹכִי אֶגְאָל: ‎5 וַיֹּאמֶר בֹּעַז בְּיוֹם־קְנוֹתְךָ הַשָּׂדֶה מִיַּד נָעֳמִי וּמֵאֵת רוּת הַמּוֹאֲבִיָּה אֵשֶׁת־הַמֵּת (קָנִיתִי) [קָנִיתָה֙] לְהָקִים שֵׁם־הַמֵּת עַל־נַחֲלָתוֹ: ‎6 וַיֹּאמֶר הַגֹּאֵל לֹא אוּכַל (לִגְאוֹל־) [לִגְאָל־]לִי פֶּן־אַשְׁחִית

no one but you to redeem *it*, and I am after you.'" And he said, "I will redeem *it*."

5 Then Boaz said, "On the day you buy the field from the hand of Naomi, you must also acquire Ruth the Moabitess, the widow of the deceased, in order to raise up the name of the deceased on his inheritance."

6 The closest relative said, "I cannot redeem *it* for myself, because I would jeopardize my own inheritance. Redeem *it* for yourself; you *may have* my right of redemption, for I cannot redeem *it*."

7 Now this was *the custom* in former times in Israel concerning the redemption and the exchange *of land* to confirm any matter: a man removed his sandal and gave it to another; and this was the *manner of* attestation in Israel.

8 So the closest relative said to Boaz, "Buy *it* for yourself." And he removed his sandal.

9 Then Boaz said to the elders and all the people, "You are witnesses today that I have bought from the hand of Naomi all that belonged to

אֶת־נַחֲלָתִי גְּאַל־לְךָ אַתָּה אֶת־גְּאֻלָּתִי כִּי לֹא־אוּכַל לִגְאֹל:
7 וְזֹאת לְפָנִים בְּיִשְׂרָאֵל עַל־הַגְּאוּלָּה וְעַל־הַתְּמוּרָה לְקַיֵּם כָּל־דָּבָר שָׁלַף אִישׁ נַעֲלוֹ וְנָתַן לְרֵעֵהוּ וְזֹאת הַתְּעוּדָה בְּיִשְׂרָאֵל:
8 וַיֹּאמֶר הַגֹּאֵל לְבֹעַז קְנֵה־לָךְ וַיִּשְׁלֹף נַעֲלוֹ:
9 וַיֹּאמֶר בֹּעַז לַזְּקֵנִים וְכָל־הָעָם עֵדִים אַתֶּם הַיּוֹם כִּי קָנִיתִי אֶת־כָּל־אֲשֶׁר לֶאֱלִימֶלֶךְ וְאֵת כָּל־אֲשֶׁר לְכִלְיוֹן וּמַחְלוֹן מִיַּד נָעֳמִי:
10 וְגַם אֶת־רוּת הַמֹּאֲבִיָּה אֵשֶׁת מַחְלוֹן קָנִיתִי לִי לְאִשָּׁה לְהָקִים שֵׁם־הַמֵּת עַל־נַחֲלָתוֹ וְלֹא־יִכָּרֵת שֵׁם־הַמֵּת מֵעִם אֶחָיו וּמִשַּׁעַר מְקוֹמוֹ עֵדִים אַתֶּם הַיּוֹם:
11 וַיֹּאמְרוּ כָּל־הָעָם אֲשֶׁר־בַּשַּׁעַר וְהַזְּקֵנִים עֵדִים יִתֵּן יְהוָה אֶת־הָאִשָּׁה הַבָּאָה אֶל־בֵּיתֶךָ כְּרָחֵל וּכְלֵאָה אֲשֶׁר בָּנוּ שְׁתֵּיהֶם אֶת־בֵּית יִשְׂרָאֵל וַעֲשֵׂה־חַיִל בְּאֶפְרָתָה וּקְרָא־שֵׁם בְּבֵית לָחֶם:
12 וִיהִי בֵיתְךָ כְּבֵית פֶּרֶץ אֲשֶׁר־יָלְדָה תָמָר לִיהוּדָה מִן־הַזֶּרַע אֲשֶׁר יִתֵּן יְהוָה לְךָ מִן־הַנַּעֲרָה הַזֹּאת:
13 וַיִּקַּח בֹּעַז אֶת־רוּת וַתְּהִי־לוֹ לְאִשָּׁה וַיָּבֹא אֵלֶיהָ וַיִּתֵּן יְהוָה לָהּ הֵרָיוֹן וַתֵּלֶד בֵּן:

Elimelech and all that belonged to Chilion and Mahlon.

10 "Moreover, I have acquired Ruth the Moabitess, the widow of Mahlon, to be my wife in order to raise up the name of the deceased on his inheritance, so that the name of the deceased will not be cut off from his brothers or from the court of his *birth* place; you are witnesses today."

11 All the people who were in the court, and the elders, said, "*We are* witnesses. May the LORD make the woman who is coming into your home like Rachel and Leah, both of whom built the house of Israel; and may you achieve wealth in Ephrathah and become famous in Bethlehem.

12 "Moreover, may your house be like the house of Perez whom Tamar bore to Judah, through the offspring which the LORD will give you by this young woman."

13 So Boaz took Ruth, and she became his wife, and he went in to her. And the

14 וַתֹּאמַרְנָה הַנָּשִׁים אֶל־נָעֳמִי בָּרוּךְ יְהֹוָה אֲשֶׁר לֹא הִשְׁבִּית לָךְ גֹּאֵל הַיּוֹם וְיִקָּרֵא שְׁמוֹ בְּיִשְׂרָאֵל:

15 וְהָיָה לָךְ לְמֵשִׁיב נֶפֶשׁ וּלְכַלְכֵּל אֶת־שֵׂיבָתֵךְ כִּי כַלָּתֵךְ אֲשֶׁר־אֲהֵבָתֶךְ יְלָדַתּוּ אֲשֶׁר־ הִיא טוֹבָה לָךְ מִשִּׁבְעָה בָּנִים:

16 וַתִּקַּח נָעֳמִי אֶת־הַיֶּלֶד וַתְּשִׁתֵהוּ בְחֵיקָהּ וַתְּהִי־לוֹ לְאֹמֶנֶת:

17 וַתִּקְרֶאנָה לוֹ הַשְּׁכֵנוֹת שֵׁם לֵאמֹר יֻלַּד־בֵּן לְנָעֳמִי וַתִּקְרֶאנָה שְׁמוֹ עוֹבֵד הוּא אֲבִי־יִשַׁי אֲבִי דָוִד: פ

18 וְאֵלֶּה תּוֹלְדוֹת פָּרֶץ פֶּרֶץ הוֹלִיד אֶת־חֶצְרוֹן:

19 וְחֶצְרוֹן הוֹלִיד אֶת־רָם וְרָם הוֹלִיד אֶת־עַמִּינָדָב:

20 וְעַמִּינָדָב הוֹלִיד אֶת־נַחְשׁוֹן וְנַחְשׁוֹן הוֹלִיד אֶת־שַׂלְמָה:

21 וְשַׂלְמוֹן הוֹלִיד אֶת־בֹּעַז וּבֹעַז הוֹלִיד אֶת־עוֹבֵד:

22 וְעֹבֵד הוֹלִיד אֶת־יִשַׁי וְיִשַׁי הוֹלִיד אֶת־דָּוִד:

LORD enabled her to conceive, and she gave birth to a son.

[14] Then the women said to Naomi, "Blessed is the LORD who has not left you without a redeemer today, and may his name become famous in Israel.

[15] "May he also be to you a restorer of life and a sustainer of your old age; for your daughter-in-law, who loves you and is better to you than seven sons, has given birth to him."

[16] Then Naomi took the child and laid him in her lap, and became his nurse.

[17] The neighbor women gave him a name, saying, "A son has been born to Naomi!" So they named him Obed. He is the father of Jesse, the father of David.

[18] Now these are the generations of Perez: to Perez was born Hezron,

[19] and to Hezron was born Ram, and to Ram, Amminadab,

[20] and to Amminadab was born Nahshon, and to Nahshon, Salmon,

<table>
<tr><td>

[21] and to Salmon was born Boaz, and to Boaz, Obed,

[22] and to Obed was born Jesse, and to Jesse, David.

</td><td></td></tr>
</table>

Process of Discovery

Linguistics Section

Linguistic Structure

A [1] Now Boaz went up to the gate and sat down there, and behold, the close relative of whom Boaz spoke was passing by, so he said, "Turn aside, friend, sit down here." And he turned aside and sat down. [2] He took ten men of the elders of the city and said, "Sit down here." So they sat down.

B [3] Then he said to the closest relative, "Naomi, who has come back from the land of Moab, has to sell the piece of land which belonged to our brother Elimelech. [4] "So I thought to inform you, saying, 'Buy *it* before those who are sitting *here*, and before the elders of my people. If you will redeem *it*, redeem *it*; but if not, tell me that I may know; for there is no one but you to redeem *it*, and I am after you.'" And he said, "I will redeem *it*."

C [5] Then Boaz said, "On the day you buy the field from the hand of Naomi, you must also acquire Ruth the Moabitess, the widow of the deceased, in order to raise up the name of the deceased on his inheritance."

B' [6] The closest relative said, "I cannot redeem *it* for myself, because I would jeopardize my own inheritance. Redeem *it* for yourself; you *may have* my right of redemption, for I cannot redeem *it*." [7] Now this was *the custom* in former times in Israel concerning the redemption and the exchange *of land* to confirm any matter: a man removed his sandal and gave it to another, and this was the *manner of* attestation in Israel. [8] So the closest relative said to Boaz, "Buy *it* for yourself." And he removed his sandal. [9] Then Boaz said to the elders and all the people, "You are witnesses today that I have bought from the hand of Naomi all that belonged to Elimelech and all that belonged to Chilion and Mahlon. [10] "Moreover, I have acquired Ruth the Moabitess, the widow of Mahlon, to be my wife in order to raise up the name of the deceased on his inheritance, so that the name of the deceased will not be cut off from his brothers or from the court of his *birth* place; you are witnesses today."

A' [11] All the people who were in the court, and the elders, said, "*We are* witnesses. May the LORD make the woman who is coming into your home like Rachel and Leah, both of whom built the house of Israel; and may you achieve wealth in Ephrathah and become famous in Bethlehem. [12] "Moreover, may your house be like the house of Perez whom Tamar bore to Judah, through the offspring which the LORD will give you by this young woman."
A [13] So Boaz took Ruth, and she became his wife, and he went in to her. And the LORD enabled her to conceive, and she gave birth to a son.

B [14] Then the women said to Naomi, "Blessed is the LORD who has not left you without a redeemer today, and may his name become famous in Israel. [15] "May he also be to you a restorer of life and a sustainer of your old age; for your daughter-in-law, who loves you and is better to you than seven sons, has given birth to him."

A' [16] Then Naomi took the child and laid him in her lap, and became his nurse. [17] The neighbor women gave him a name, saying, "A son has been born to Naomi!" So they named him Obed. He is the father of Jesse, the father of David.

[Genealogy of Perez] [18] Now these are the generations of Perez: to Perez was born Hezron, [19] and to Hezron was born Ram, and to Ram, Amminadab, [20] and to Amminadab was born Nahshon, and to Nahshon, Salmon, [21] and to Salmon was born Boaz, and to Boaz, Obed, [22] and to Obed was born Jesse, and to Jesse, David.

Discussion

This chapter tells the narrative of the marriage of Ruth and Boaz.

Questioning the Passage

1. What does it mean to redeem the land? (v. 4)

   To redeem the land is to purchase it. Boaz wanted the land purchased so that it stayed inside of the family

2. What does verse five mean?

   The person who purchases the land from Naomi had to take Ruth as his wife. Their children would be Ruth's first husband's children so that any inherited land would stay within the family.

Culture Section

Discussion

The gates of a city were the place to gather and talk. The judges for the city would be at the gate, and any disputes were brought before them. Boaz gathered ten men who were his relatives to talk to them about what he should do with Naomi and Ruth.

Questioning the passage

1. Why did Boaz remove a shoe in verse seven?

   "In the Near East when the hand of a girl was sought in marriage and the father was willing to give her in marriage, he would say; "'I will make her a pair of shoes and place her under your feet.'"[19]

Thoughts

As Boaz contemplated marrying Ruth, he did not forget his cultural obligations. It was important that a child was born to Ruth so that the inheritance of her dead husband would stay inside of the family. Family obligations were very important to the people living in ancient days. The land each person

---

[19] Rocco A. Errico and George M. Lamsa, *Aramaic Light on Joshua Through 2 Chronicles* (Smyma, GA: Noohra Foundation, 2009).

received was a gift from the LORD. He promised the people the land. Therefore, the people considered the land sacred, and it was mandatory that the Torah laws about inheritance be obeyed.

Reflections

Sometimes it is clear that people today are not as concerned about family honor and inheritance. Children move away from parents because they do not like the area in which their parents' lived or the need to move because of employment. In ancient times the nuclear family stayed together. Taking care of the family is a primary task of the Hebrew people.

Bibliography

n.d. *Boaz.* Accessed May 10, 2019.

> http://www.aboutbibleprophecy.com/p153.htm.

Davis, Anne Kimball. 2012. *The Synoptic Gospels.*

Errico, Rocco A. 2009. *Aramaic Light on Joshua Through 2 Cnronicles.* Smyrna: GA: Noohra Foundation.

1986. *Back to School.* Directed by Paper Clip Productions.

Scherman, Meir Zlotowitz and Nosson. 1993. *The Five Megillos: A New Translation with a Commentary Anthologized from Talmudic, Midrashic, and Rabbinic Sources.* New York: New York: Mesorah Publications.

n.d. *The Bible Journey: Ruth's Journey to Bethlehem.* Accessed May 07, 2019.

> https://www.thebiblejourney.org/biblejourney2/29-the-journeys-of-ruth-and-samuel/ruths-journey-to-bethlehem.

End notes

---

[i] Rabbi Solomon ben Isaac (Shlomo Yitzhaki), known as Rashi (based on an acronym of his Hebrew initials), is one of the most influential Jewish commentators in history. He was born in Troyes, Champagne, in northern France, in 1040. Source: https://www.myjewishlearning.com/article/who-was-rashi/

www.ingramcontent.com/pod-product-compliance
Lightning Source LLC
Chambersburg PA
CBHW051246160726
47994CB00003B/1039